This Book is dedicated to Sirpa, who just gets the Pelonteet.

Hotti Meets Pelonteet

Hotti and the Pelonteet treasure chest

Hotti and the Pelonteet loss of leaves

Teija Autio

Hotti Meets Pelonteet

PELONTEET

EST. 2018

Publisher: BoD – Books on Demand, Helsinki, Suomi / Finland
Manufacturer: BoD – Books on Demand, Norderstedt, Saksa

ISBN: 978-952-80-6052-9

Pelonteet in this Book

You do know everything we people go through,

Small and vast thoughts inside our head, false or true.

Now you see some things with a twist of light,

You could even get a brand-new insight!

In this book you're holding right now,

Is Hotti waiting for you, maybe even to make you go wow!

Journey will take us through some fears and feeling,

With the help of Pelonteet so thrilling.

Please keep an open mind from now on,

cause mind is the **Pelonteet** kingdom.

HOTTI

This here is Hotti, that's for sure.

See, the character, innocent and pure.

But the greatest gift in Hotti is surely that,

the **openness** of the mind and heart so vast.

Now you shall hear a dreamy story,

With light and softness, not with glory.

This story was painted for Hotti's mind,

To show the goodness in Pelonteet-kind.

Now we will turn the page with roar,

We have a Pelonteet-world to explore!!

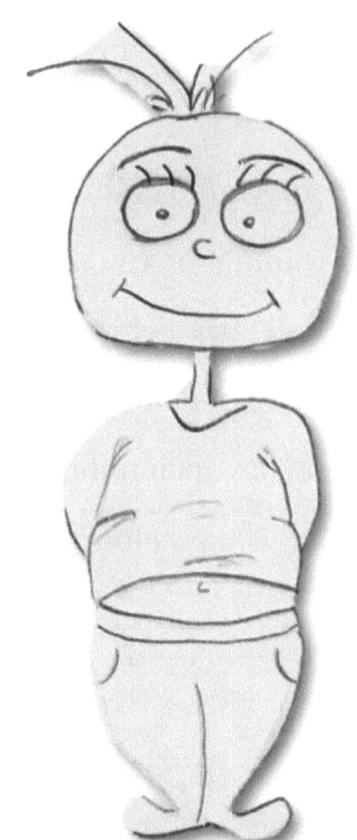

Hotti

DARKIESTUFF PELONNE

Hotti peeks under the bed, almost like a cave,

Unbelievable, there is a new **friend** giving a wave.

There's no fear in Hotti's vast soul,

Only warm joy of a new friend with a glow.

"Who are you", Hotti whispers.

"Glo is my name", Glo answers.

Glo

Indark

WEIRDNESS PELONNE

First thought came flying into Hotti's mind
Am I nuts or some of that kind?

Pelonne beside him, star upon,
Smiles and laughes, pointing on.

"You're not weird, not even close crazy,
It just might feel for start a little bit hazy!"

"Let me introduce you, to a new friend.
Hello Wacky", Glo called and waved.

Wacky
Weirdo

JUDGECRITICISM PELONNE

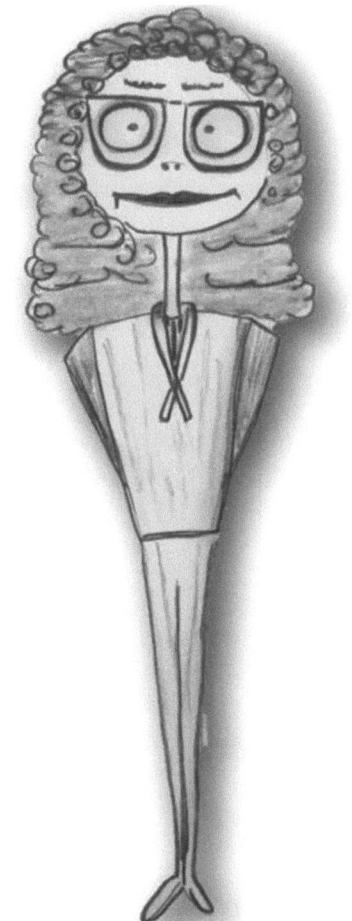

**Judgy
Von Judgersson**

Suddenly a shadow passed sadly-bloomy,

Hotti's face darkened and became gloomy.

Glo noticed the mood change,

And straight away spoke ahead:

"So we meet again with your stiffness-

Pelonne Judgecriticism – none the less"

Below the rigid appearance though,

Judgy wishes love all and around:

"Please **don't judge anyone** with no reason,

That's a sure way to your mind's prison!"

ETERNAL UNEMPLOYMENT PELONNE

"What a great job Judgy had,

Hotti pondered a little sad.

What if I don't have work,

Am I then useless, just like a broken fork?"

Then made its entrance a goody bag,

Hey, it's **Suupussi**, not too shag!

"There are many ways to work in world,

Some even stayin' up late worth!

Please follow me now", Suupussi asks,

Warmth and love from its bag spreads.

Suupussi

LOVECENTRUM EQUILIBRIUM PELONNE

Laavjing Juujang,

Pelonne Beautiful of the Realm,

Flickering with the hearts

of the dresses' hem.

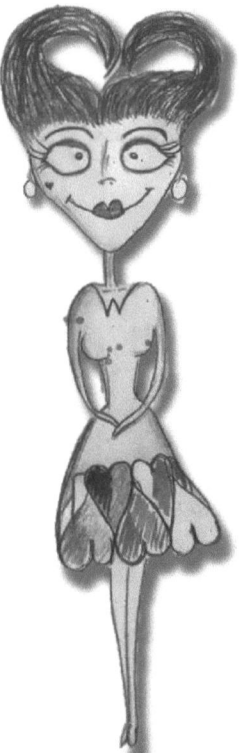

Laavjing

Juujang

Brings **balance** to all around,

Bestows love forever and to all ground.

Company around Hotti felt like fairytale,

Suddenly he felt anxiety and became pale.

What if they abandon me,

Leaving me totally alone, you see?

ABANDONMENT PELONNE

Glo comforted and shrugged,

Tightly Hotti he hugged.

"Nobody's going to abandon you,

We are with you, that is so true."

Hotti on the edge of the deepest fears,

Glimpsed nice new Pelonne and shed no tears.

Abnis

Abhylky

"Abnis it just is, Suupussi smiling stated.

Warm hug they shared above the chest plated.

NONEXITHINGY PELONNE

Next new friend was named Eet:

"**Non-edible** are all the Pelonteet!"

When you are aware of existence,

You'll be given pure love, no fence!"

These words lightened Hotti's heart,

And so continued this journey's part.

Eet

Minot

KNOWCANDO PELONNE

"Many studies and knowledge does the world offer,

Don't take everything as truth, like the otter!

You know something or you don't,

You enjoy life, with **unique font**.

We have happiness inside, in each of us.

We have the same beingness in our core thus."

Len

Happi Onmii

TIMEFLOW PELONNE

Hotti pondered and wondered.

Kept thinking and blinking.

Who is speaking, and with what mouth,

Where is North and where is South?

"On the same land we live and be–

The same air we all **breathe**.

Can I hear the wheel of time chewing fuss,

Making an end of the humanity in us?"

NowU

Livhere

MEANSYMBOLILLISM PELONNE

Glo softly nudged very close:

"Try not to overthink – or dose!"

You can put everything neatly

in folders and bins

 put a sticker on firmly

on all the things

But the unlimited freedom of being phase,

is a wonderful, **unqualified case!**

"Let's go cool off, you say what?

I know the best place for that!"

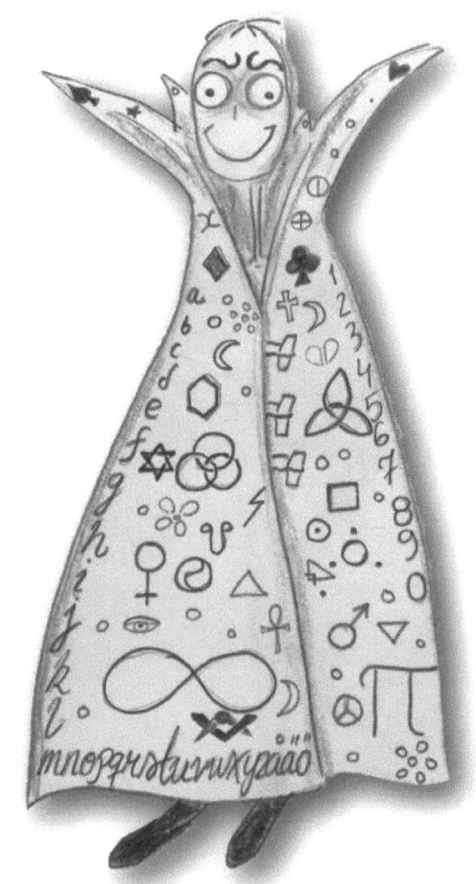

De

Cipher

SOLOMELTARMLESS PELONNE

So, they journeyed,

And finally reached the end.

Oh, how hilarious it was to see,

Coolest **snowman** in the freeze.

"I think you'll never melt down,

You are the mightiest Pelonne in the subzero town!!"

Snou

Loneblower

SUBCONSCHANGLING PELONNE

From cold back to hot,

Alone they were yet again not-

Disso gave them one advice wise,

"Watch always with **truthful** eyes."

When you comprehend this without any trouble,

It is sooo fine to also spend time in a bubble.

Everything about yourself can be a story,

Your thoughts affect the world- that's inventory!

Be present here and now,

That's a sensitive wow!

DisSo
DoNot

BUBBELDUBBELCOVER PELONNE

"That's right, indeed,

we have the most awesome mind,

Amazing colour feed,

and unique to each kind."

When you realize this and underline double,

It's fine to float around in a **bubble**.

AB.Out

Topop

Suddenly Hotti heard time ticking,

Small hours felt itching under the skin.

Thoughts of Hotti circulating,

Will I meet Pelonteet never again.

So soon are we at the end of times,

What becomes of me, of **all** the chimes?

Glo stayed beside Hotti, glowing, leaping:

"Just use the AM hours wisely, sleeping!

They are just Pelonteet **flying** around,

Thoughts like clouds passing by pound."

Rats AM

Twinxthinks

DECISIONDONKING PELONNE

A8kmii

Hotti catched something off the ground,
It was nice, all black and round.

Deeply thinking
without blinking.

Soon he met only one eye,
"**Take it easy**, you know why.

Now roll-on with me to meet,
Ican, our inside one-superhero-fleet!"

INNERMOST PELONNE

New buddies were gladly met,

Hands were shaken wet

Ican Survive plus Con Nected

Joined the suite unexpected.

"So, when you feel inside the freeing,

power of your true **innermost** being,

You'll see it very soon,

Face the truth under the moon! "

Ican

Survive

UNITEDUNIQUENESS PELONNE

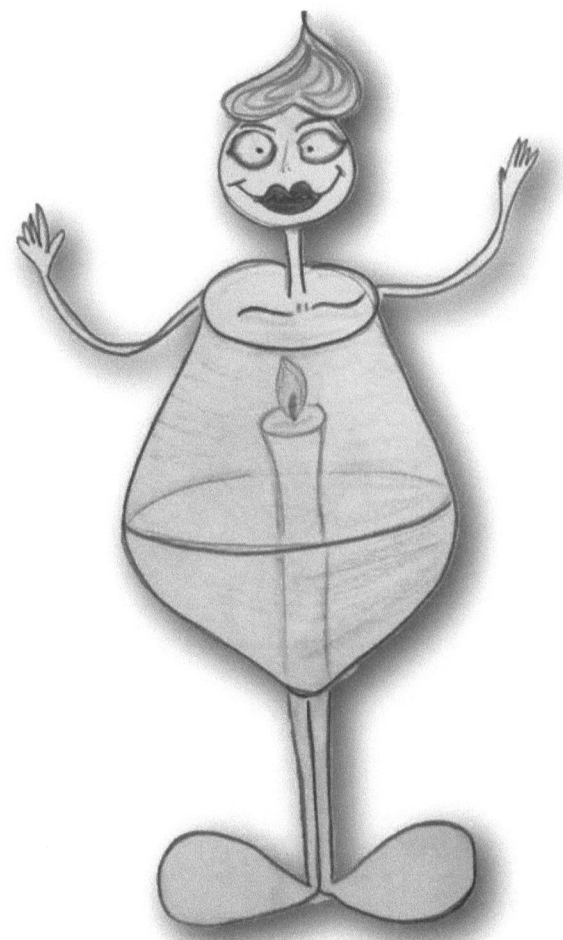

"Hmm, I think I start to realize",
Hotti almost whispered with closed eyes.

We are all the same in essence,
All we have something in **common** as sense.

Pelonne next shines so softly,
candle burning in the dome off me.

Con
Nected

SPIRSOULENLIGHT PELONNE

Hotti almost the enlightenment reached,

But then, like suddenly ceded.

SORROGRIEVING PELONNE

"This is trying to weigh me down really low,

We are not becoming nothing but old?

Sorrow, grievance, and tears

And in the end only old people fears!"

Tear

Dropplop

LIFEBEGGIN' PELONNE

W. Heat

de Grainy

OLDIESTUFF PELONNE

"There is nothing to fear in old age,

See the **sweetness** of Hermeseta on this page.

Everything becomes soft,

on the other hand, tough,

I guarantee this croft:

you are the gentlest without bluff!

So live care-free throughout your life,

You can even marry-barry a husband or a wife."

Hermeseta

Inkontin

"Hermy"

SEEMWISES PELONNE

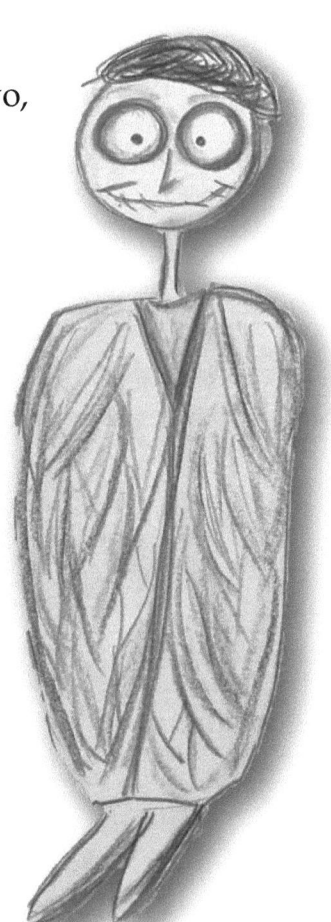

The **life's** beggars are trying to teach us a lesson or two,

But I don't know if pure wisdom is even true??

"Is wise he who is silent, no anxiety

or he that doeth nothing quietly?"

Knowowl

Nothing

DEATHSENDY PELONNE

Hotti stayed a little worried still,

Asking and stuttering out loud the will:

"What if I fear indeed the last breath

The end of it all, I mean d e a t h?"

"Why fear the unknown,

Thing, which none of us really know?

Breathe Hotti, and **Love** as much as you can,

I'll be jumping around, like a sticking pan."

Bunnybury calmed Hotti down,

Heart-paws glittering in red and brown.

Bunnybury
Up

WEIGHPUT PELONNE

Beautiful wild field together

they cross, quietly in shield forever-

heat of it in their cells and veins,

Pelonteet and Hotti feel, are ripe grains.

Finally they arrive in the woods of Soul.

Just a moment still, small hours go on.

They sit around a big rock.

"Am I seeing a new friend there, or is it a mock?"

Hotti is very tranquil and yawning,

Pelonteet are all around, smiling.

Light
S. Tone

FALLFLOATING PELONNE

This all was so wonderful and thrilling, dude,

Hotti closes eyes, heart filled with gratitude.

Like with feathers wings Pelonteet hum,

Go To sleep, human child, lullaby beats like a drum.

Fea
Ther

Happily Ever After. 😊

To be continued...

To My Family.